WE ANIMALS WOULD LIKE A WORD WITH YOU

John Agard

Illustrated by
Satoshi Kitamura

RED FOX

For Kalera
and her kitten

A Red Fox Book

Published by Random House Children's Books
20 Vauxhall Bridge Road, London SW1V 2SA

A division of Random House UK Ltd
London Melbourne Sydney Auckland
Johannesburg and agencies throughout the world

First published simultaneously in hardback and paperback by
The Bodley Head Children's Books and Red Fox 1996

Printed and bound in Belgium by
Proost International Book Production

Papers used by Random House UK Ltd are natural, recyclable products
made from wood grown in sustainable forests. The manufacturing
processes conform to the environmental regulations of the country of
origin.

RANDOM HOUSE UK Limited Reg. No. 954009

ISBN 0 09 968851 4

Contents

Rat Race

Rat race?
Don't make us laugh.
It's you humans
who're always in a haste.

Ever seen a rat
in a bowler hat
rushing to catch a train?

Ever seen a rat
with a briefcase
hurrying through the rain?

And isn't it a fact
that all that hurry-hurry
gives you humans heart attacks?

No, my friend,
we rats relax.

Pass the cheese,
please.

Frog Hop

I may be ugly
but I have my hop.

I have no wish
to be kissed
and turned
to a prince

and mince
along
in awkward
finery.

Me? Abandon
my kingdom
of wet and weed
and insect feast?

Oh keep your kiss.
Oh keep your prince
dressed like a fop.

I'll keep my hop.

Elephants Dreaming

On a marvellous grey morning
A mountain is beginning to breathe.
Each rock shudders with long memories.
The sun blows her yellow trumpet
Over a hunter asleep with his gun.
O what a beautiful day for a stampede.

Hare I Am

Of course I'm Hare.
Where else will I be
but here, there, everywhere.

In woods. In bogs.
In reeds of marsh
mad as March

I rise. I set
on leap-light paws
in moon-marked air.
So when you hunt me down
with hounding dogs
and tear my skin asunder.

Remember, gentlemen,
you've just murdered
the moon's ambassador.

Hippo Writes
A Love Poem to
his Wife

Oh my beautiful fat wife
Larger to me than life
Smile broader than the river Nile
My winsome waddlesome
You do me proud in the shallow of morning
You do me proud in the deep of night
Oh, my bodysome mud-basking companion.

Hippo Writes
A Love Poem to her
Husband

Oh my lubby-dubby hubby-hippo
With your widely-winning lippo
My Sumo-thrasher of water
Dearer to me than any two-legger
How can I live without
Your ponderful potamus pout?

The Little Fish has something

Throw down your hook
you silly man
throw down your hook.

I can read you like a book.

Guess you've heard
of a school of fish?
Well, I was the brightest
in my class
and my teacher always said
whenever you see a hook
just pass.

Throw down your hook
you silly man
throw down your hook.

You won't catch a thing
in this river
we're far too clever.

o say to the Fisherman...

At least you won't catch me
I wanna go to university
for fish, man,

not end up in your frying-pan.

Sir Grizzly

My name
is Bear

Sir Grizzly
to you.
Endear-
Endear-
Ingly
Cuddly
But beware.
I instil
Fear
And can kill
With a hug.

Come closer
My good man.
Have we been introduced?

I am dying
To shake your hand.

Circus Lion Gives Evidence

At crack of whip
I jumped through
hoops of fire.
And the people loved it.

All that clapping.
All those lights
just for me, a king
who did as he was told.
One day each clap became a roar
that filled my ear.
Each light fell
like a moon on a forest floor.
My mane flared
with old remembrances
till I was full of
myself. Full of Lion.

Then, ladies and gentlemen,
came the final trick.
And you know the rest.
At blast of trumpet
he put his head into
the kingdom of my mouth
which I closed forever.

He was a good man, my trainer.

Swimming Teeth

I'm not a do-as-you're-told fish.
A looked-at-in-a-bowl fish.
A stay-still-to-behold fish.
An as-you-can-guess goldfish.

Where sea is blue, I make it red.
Where body bubbles, I slash, I shred.
Where eyes see light, I blur them dark.
Where skin shines bright, I expose a heart.

Humans call me shark.
But to my friends of the deep
I am known as SWIMMING TEETH.
And one day I'd like to direct a movie.

Mrs Skunk Writes a Letter to the Press

Dear Editor

My husband and I were very upset
by a suggestion in your paper
that we skunks have bad breath.
You humans seem to forget
the dirty wind you let off
especially after you've gorged on beans.
And what about the smell of death
you bring to our rivers
from the fumes of your factories?
Humans have such short memories.
My husband and I both agreed
that your comment was most unfair.
What you humans call bad breath
We skunks call wee defensive warfare.
We're only protecting ourselves, you hear.

Yours Very Upset

Goldfish

From this position
in my bowl
of glass
I watch time pass
like food crumbs falling
slow.

Faces come.
Faces go.
Some stare at me.
I watch the children grow.
I'm part of the family.
Once they moved my bowl
closer to the telly.

Reflections

Reminded me of the sea
   except for all the noise
   and the running.

   When they moved
   me back
   to my spot by the
   curtain
   I didn't feel so sad
   then.
   Kept thinking
   we're all in one big
   bowl.
   They live in a bowl too.

Thinking Turtle

I'm the thinking turtle
Known to all as the thinker of the shell.
And I can't help thinking:
Poor humans, they're not doing too well.

If it isn't sun burning them,
It's rain wetting them from head to toe.
And I pity the tired one
Walking his way in the snow

Oh how can they leave their house behind?
A shell like mine would suit them fine.
Humans with a shell for a back
Hurrying everywhere till they crack.

The Ants Inspect

On ant-light

steps

...we trek

...we trek

we architects

of ant-hills

ant-tunnels

ant-palaces

ant-towers

here we come

in our armies of

crawling millions

to inspect

inspect

what human

hands erect

The Spiders cast their spell

Break our
web
Break our
universe

                              We in return
will bless
you with a curse

May your two legs
grow to be eight

                              May your sleep be
too light
for the weight
of your dreams

May your house
collapse
at the slight
touch of a breeze

                              And as you sit
among the ruin
of your memories

May you wish
for thread to spin
May you wish
for thread to spin

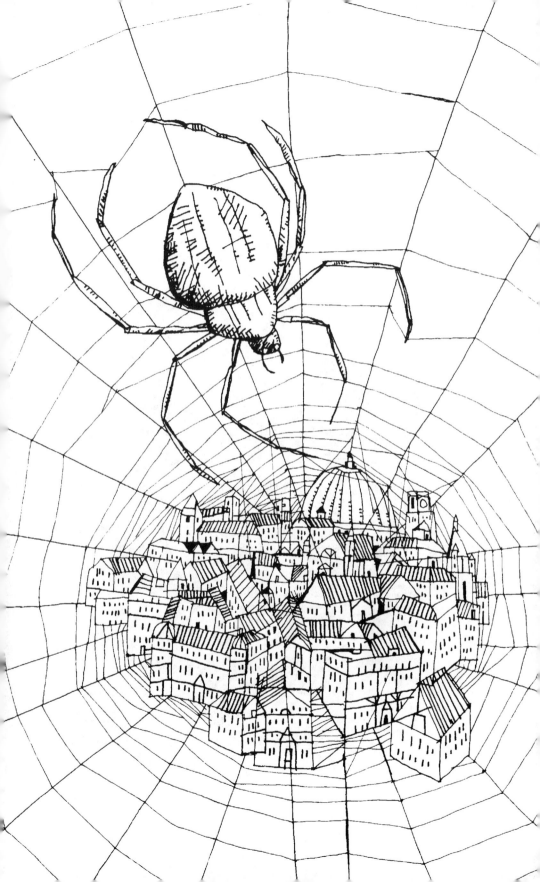

Tigers' Graffiti

Another Word From Frog

Look at little me
curled under a log

If I said a mountain
grew out of my navel

Would you grin
Would you marvel

Would you stare like me
Eyes all agog?

A Reminder from Snake

Slitheringly slimy
Creepingly crawly
Potently poisonous
Viciously venomous

Fine words indeed
you use to describe us.
But do we snakes need
to jolt your memory?

Where would you be
if Eve didn't listen
to our ancestor -
Most Marvellous Snake?

You'd still be all alone
in the Garden of Eden.
No kids. No home.
No clothes. No telephone.

Telling it Like a Pig

We've heard it all before
DON'T EAT LIKE A PIG,
PIGS ARE DIRTY and more.
But we eat no more than folks scoff.

We pigs will let you know
the reason why we wallow.
We wallow to rid our skins
of parasites that itch and bite.

Do you get what we mean?
In other words, to keep clean.
And just for your information,
long long ago in a fairy kingdom

We pigs were bearers of wisdom.

Insects Masquerade

Bet you didn't know
a broken twig could grow
two sudden wings
and take off to the sky?
Unless you're a clever moth
camouflaged like a spy.

Bet you'd never guess
a thread
dangling
high
could begin
to
squirm.
That's me, Inchworm.

So you thought
I was a stick?
Until you tried to pick
me up. Then too quick
for your hands was I.

What a surprise
when you realized
I was no dry leaf
But a butterfly
making a fool of your eyes.

When will you humans learn
that we insects love disguise.

The Homing Pigeon
Thinks of The Lost Explorer

Look at him.
Poor chap.
Lost without his map.

Day for him
has become night.
What a stumbling sight.

Heading north
and hoping south.
Hear him shout.
His voice is lost.
And food like time
is running out.

See me homing
as pigeons do.
Empress of the blue.

On wind-waves I ride
ever homing homing
in pigeon pride.

I can guide him
to the horizon's rim.
Poor chap with no map,

Trust me.

Bats advice

Looking at life
from upside down
with your feet
to the sky
and your face
to the ground
you may ponder
the question
of how and why
and where you're from.
Make night your day
and day your night.
Bless the world
from upside down.

Crocodile's Tale

The last man who mistook me for a log
Lost half-a-foot and can no longer jog.

A Conference of Cows

Here munching grass
Watching time pass

Chewing our cud
No thoughts of blood

Under us green
Above us blue

Welcome little words
like love and moo

HopalooKangaroo

If you can jigaloo
jigaloo
I can do
the jigaloo too
for I'm the jiggiest
jigaloo kangaroo

    jigaloo all night through
    jigaloo all night through

If you can boogaloo
boogaloo
I can do
the boogaloo too
for I'm the boogiest
boogaloo kangaroo

    boogaloo all night through
    boogaloo all night through

But bet you can't hopaloo
hopaloo
like I can do
for I'm the hoppiest
hopaloo kangaroo

hopaloo all night through
hopaloo all night through

Gonna show you steps
you never knew.
And guess what, guys?
My baby in my pouch
will be dancing too.

Bedbugs
Marching
Song

Bedbugs

Have the right

To bite.

Bedbugs

Of the world

Unite.

Don't let

These humans

Sleep too tight.

Space Dog Remembers

First dog in orbit
and proud of it.
But was scared, must admit

Felt trapped
in a kennel of air.
My cry lost among a million spheres.

Kept wishing every minute
Would return to earth soon.
Couldn't bring myself to bark at moon.

No dog smell among the clouds.
No ball to chase. No stick.
What's the good wagging at a planet?

My paws longed for sand or grass.
Preferred the park to a sputnik.
But raised my hind legs out of habit.

Return to earth was the best bit.
Was given marvellous doggie biscuit.
My picture on every front page.

Now in paw-licking old age
I ask myself, was it worth it?

But I am man's best friend.
On earth, on moon, wherever
I will wag his welcome to the end.

I have a home.
I have a bone.
A tale to tell.

The last Bird

I am becoming
the last bird
on the last branch
of the last tree
about to disappear
from the face of the earth.

The trees my friends, all gone.
Only empty holes
where trees used to be.
No more leaves to share
my secrets. All gone.
I am becoming
the last bird...

Suddenly, I wake
to a shake of wind.
I feel Mama's wing
her comforting beak
her feather-cosy breast.
Ah lucky me,
I'm safe in my nest.
Was only having a little bird's nightmare.

Yet why do I turn
again and again
as if waiting to hear
the deathly fall
of
a green-stealing rain?

Oh Mama
wing me
with your love.

Donkey's Couplet

You're the one with the whip. You're the boss.
But I'm the one whose back bears the Cross.

Owl

Why does night rest its gourd in my
breast?
Why does the moon puff out my
feathers?
Why do mice twinkle like stars?
Why does the darkness hoot in my
ears?
Why does a hollow tree seem like
heaven?
I am so bespectacled with questions,
The poor fools call it wisdom.

Cat's Note

How often can you take a poem
and stroke it on your lap?

Whale in shape

Who says I am overweight?
I am the great beluga whale
I flap my God-almighty tail.

It feels rumptiously great
when my blubber meets the billows.
I love it when my fat takes the sea-blows.
And listen to this, fellows.
Bet I can triple-flip my tail
faster than you can touch your toes.

I have no use for your bathroom scale.

Camel's Invitation

Touch my hump
and the desert
will linger on your hands

Look into
the good book of my eyes
And you will see a star
in the east
where the wise ones sit

Cradle the beast
that kneels on sand
and you will feel
such a beautiful thirst

From this day on
you will walk with your lips
to the sky

What a Shame
You Lost Your Tail

'What a shame
you humans
lost your tail,' said Monkey.

You could have been doing like me
and swinging from tree to tree.

'What a shame
you humans
lost your tail,' said Dog.

Now, that's a drag,
when friends come you got nothing to wag.

'What a shame
you humans
lost your tail,' said Lizard.

If I break mine, no bother,
I can always grow back another.

'What a shame
you humans
lost your tail,' said Coyote.

In the beginning when fire was rare and earth dark,
it was my tricky brush that stole the magic spark.

'What a shame
you humans
lost your tail,' said Anaconda.

When I crush a body till the final squeal,
what a joy to coil myself around my meal.

'What a shame
you humans
lost your tail,' said Pig.

My curly stump,
sure adds a touch to my old rump.

'What a shame
you humans
lost your tail,' said Beaver.

Moving through water is easy to handle
When you're born with a ready-made paddle.

'We know
we lost our tail,' said the humans.

But we have a bottom, a bum, a rear,
call it what you will.
It's good for sitting on
to improve our thinking skill.

'Yes, we lost our tail,'
said the humans once again.
'But we have a brain
and we make things that heal and things

that kill.'

I am the ambassador of the moon, and this is what the god says to you by my mouth...

(Voice of the Hare from
an Indian Folk-tale)